INTRODUCTION

MW00790084

Swapna Nidra Gnyana Sadhana, the ¹ an intense self-exploration and one should not expect that by reading the book once, the Supreme Truth will be instantly revealed.

Truth Realization sets its own pre-requisite: The old conditioning of 'I dream, I sleep' needs to be erased to reveal the background Reality. This erasure is in itself a Sadhana.

This Sadhana is a simple 6-step process:

Step 1] Unlike a novel, read one page and ponder over it.

Step 2] Attempt to comprehend each word. It is not unknown. The inner knowing is merely masked.

Step 3] Allow the Flow to reveal the Truths as the physical body retires for the night. Unveiling the mask of the Waker is an important phenomenon that occurs naturally.

Step 4] Allow Dream and Sleep to reveal deeper Truths.

Step 5] Have the courage to acknowledge the revealed Truth until conviction matures.

Step 6] Abide in the Truth!

Only on the revelation that you are not the Waker does an internal shift manifest. Being ephemeral in nature, it requires astute attention. An extended marination in the New Seeing may be in order.

Without this step, you will remain ever confused. Truth is easily veiled by illusion. Only you can work your way out of your illusion as it is caused by your own past conditioning and belief.

Therefore, never begin from your belief of 'I am the body-mind-person'. Begin from the openness that emerges from the readiness to embrace the Unknown. Allowing the unknown to reveal your nature of Being Beyond is an essential requirement.

Start with a reminder every night that you are not the body-mind that sleeps. You are not that which is awake. You are NOT. Start with this subtle intention, 'May the True Nature be revealed'.

To See, you must dedicate yourself to Swapna Nidra Gnyana Sadhana. Every quote in this book leaves room for you to make your personal notes. When you 'See', make a note. Do not stop until you really See that, 'You are not the Waker. You are not the body-mind-person. You are beyond'.

Merely believing my words will not get you there.

See it.

Embrace it.

It will soon reveal that you are not the Dreamer either. Major Milestone accomplished!

Then follows the most important work: Revelation of the Truth of Deep Sleep.

Be aware of the tremendous resistance from the identification as the 'person'. It will try to override your new Seeing of Deep Sleep. You must now allow the deeply embedded belief to shed away and recognize that 'You are not the sleeper, you never were. You have never slept. You cannot sleep. Only the body-mind disappear. Their absence has been termed as sleep'. This recognition will exonerate you from the shackles of Conditioning.

If you are a 'Truth Aspirant' and have an authentic yearning to find the answer to the question 'Who Am I', you are at the right place.

Begin your Sadhana today and do not stop until you recognize the following:
You are not the Waker.
You are not the Dreamer.
You are not the Sleeper.
You are not a spiritual seeker.
You are not yearning for liberation.
YOU ARE NOT because there is no YOU.

Do not stop until the 'I' totally dissolves. There is no 'I', there is no 'You', there is no 'World'.

Then what is?

Turn the page to commence your journey.

THE SADHANA

Refrain from translating 'Sadhana' as a 'Practice'.

Sadhana is the complete Effacement of conditioning.

Effacement cannot be cultivated.

It is simply a natural release borne of 'Direct Seeing'.

So go on, See the truth while refraining from blind belief.

THE SADHANA

Start with the recognition that, right in this moment, you are able to notice that you are the witness of the eyes reading these words.

You abide beyond the body.

Take a moment to hold the stand of the beyond.

Then proceed forwards...

I Am The Witness Of The Person. [1]

I Witness
That I Am Not The
Person. [2]

I Witness
That The Body-Mind
Person Operates
Automatically Without
My Support. [3]

I Witness
That I
Falsely Claim Ownership
Of Actions. [4]

I Witness
That I
Falsely Claim Ownership
Of Thoughts. [5]

I Witness
That I
Falsely Claim Ownership
Of Feelings. [6]

I Witness
That I Falsely Claim
Doership And
Experiencership. [7]

I Witness
The Waking State In
Which There Is A Waker
In A Waking World. [8]

I Witness
That The Waker Is Not
Different From The
Waking State Itself.
There Is No Separate
Waking State From The
Waker. [9]

I Witness
That The
Waking Person =
Perception + Sensation +
Thought + Feeling. [10]

I Witness
That The Waker Is Not
Constantly Perceived.
There Are Gaps Of
Absence Of
The Waker. [11]

I Witness
That The Waking State Is
Not Constantly
Perceived.
There Are Gaps Of
Absence Sandwiched In
Between Two Waking
Recognitions. [12]

I Witness
The Waker And The
Waking State As One.
I Am Beyond Both. [13]

I Witness
The Dream State
In Which
There Is A Dream
Subject
In A Dream World. [14]

I Witness
That The Dream State Is
Not Different From The
Dream Subject In A
Dream World. [15]

I Witness
That The Dream Person
And The Waking Person
Are Never Perceived
Simultaneously. [16]

I Witness
That The Dream
Vanishes On Being
Witnessed. [17]

I Witness
That
The Dream Is Similar To
The Waking Perceptions,
Sensations, Thoughts
And Feelings. [18]

I Witness
That
There Is A Gap Between
Two Dreams. [19]

I Witness
That There Is A
Continuity In Dream
Stories Just Like There Is
A Continuity In The
Waking Story. [20]

I Witness
That The Waking And
Dream States Are Not
Different. They Are
Identical. [21]

I Witness
That I Do Not Need
Sense Organs To Perceive
The Dream World. Could
This Apply To The
Waking As Well? [22]

I Witness
That The Belief, 'The
Dream World Is Based
On Memories Of The
Waking World' Is Not
Completely True. [23]

I Am The Witness
Of Both The Waking
And The Dream. I Am
Beyond Both. [24]

I Witness That
The Waker Is
Absent In The
Deep Sleep State. [25]

I Witness
That The Dreamer Is
Absent In The Deep
Sleep State. [26]

I Witness
The Darkness Of
Absence Of The Waking
And Dream Worlds. [27]

I Witness
That When I Renounce
The Assumption That
'I Am Absent In Deep
Sleep', I Recognize My
True Nature. [28]

I Witness
That The Absence
Reveals The Truth Of
My Formlessness.
Only I Am. [29]

I Witness
That I Am Limitless.
There Is No Form
To Limit Me. [30]

I Witness
That The Waker
[That Is Absent In Deep
Sleep] Provides The
Proof Of
The Bliss Of
Deep Sleep. [31]

I Witness That
The Dreamer
[That Is Absent In Deep
Sleep]
Also Provides The Proof
Of The Bliss Of Deep
Sleep. [32]

I Witness
That I Am The Limitless
And Formless Bliss Of
The Deep Sleeper. [33]

I-The-Turiya
Am The Ceaseless
Witness Of The Three
States.
There Cannot Be A
Practice To Witness. [34]

I Am The Witness
Of The Waker,
Of The Dreamer,
Of The Deep Sleeper.
I Am The Fourth
[Turiya]. [35]

I-The-Turiya
Intermittently Forget My
True Nature And Identify
With The Waker,
Dreamer Or The Deep
Sleeper. [36]

I-The-Turiya
Appear From The
Background Of
Nothingness And
Disappear Back Into It.
Hence I Am Beyond
Turiya [Turiyatita]. [37]

My Reality Is The
Background Of
Nothingness.
I Only Assume The
Stands Of The Waker,
Dreamer, Deep Sleeper,
and Turiya
Temporarily. [38]

Is It Possible
That I Assume To Be
The Sleeper, Hence I
Experience The Total
Ignorance Of My True
Self? [39]

Is It Possible
That I Project The
Darkness Of Deep
Sleep? [40]

Is It Possible
That I Assume To Be
The Dreamer And
Therefore I Experience
The Dream World? [41]

Is It Possible
That I Project The
Dream Perceptions +
Sensations + Thoughts +
Feelings Out From The
Preceding Darkness Of
Deep Sleep? [42]

Is It Possible
Sight, Sound, Smell,
Taste, And Touch Are
Dream Perceptions
Extended To The
Waking? [43]

Is It Possible
That The Subject Is A
Figment Of Imagination
Before It Extends To
The Waking? [44]

Isn't It True
That Earth, Water, Fire,
Air, And Space Are
Dream Perceptions That
Were Absent In Deep
Sleep? [45]

Isn't It True
That The Dream Is A
Figment Of Imagination
Borne Of Deep Sleep
Darkness? [46]

Isn't It Possible
That Earth, Water, Fire,
Air, And Space Are
Dream Perceptions
Extended To The
Waking? [47]

Is It Possible
That I Assume To Be
The Waker Hence I
Experience The Waking
World? [48]

Is It Possible
That I Expand The
Dream To The Waking
Out Of
Imagination? [49]

Is It Possible
That There Is No World
Out There But Merely
Imagined Desires And
Fears Playing On A
Screen? [50]

Is It Possible That
Ignorance Of Turiya
Nurtures Identification
While Turiya Realization
Effaces It? [51]

If I Were Content
With The Pleasure Of
Dreams,
Would I Trade It For The
Waker-Identity? [52]

If I Were Content
With The Pleasure Of
Dreams,
Would I Trade It For The
Sleeper-Identity? [53]

If I Were Content
With The Pleasure Of
Sleep,
Would I Trade It For The
Waker-Identity? [54]

If I Were Content
With The Pleasure Of
Sleep, Would I Trade It
For The Dreamer-
Identity? [55]

If I Were Content
With The Pleasure Of
Waking,
Would I Trade It For The
Sleeper-Identity? [56]

If I Were Content
With The Pleasure Of
Waking,
Would I Trade It For The
Dreamer-Identity? [57]

Is There Any Pleasure
That Can Be Obtained
From Either The Waking,
Dreaming, Or The Deep
Sleep States? [58]

Isn't The Cause Of
Suffering Simply The
Search For The
Impossible Pleasure? [59]

Isn't Waking, Dream And Deep Sleep Simply Suffering For Turiya Due To Its Forgotten Nature? [60]

If I Am Real,
I Must Have Continuous
Abidance.
Can The Real Be The
Waker Now And The
Dreamer Later? [61]

If I Am Real,
I Must Have Continuous
Abidance.
Can The Real Be The
Waker Now And The
Sleeper Later? [62]

Desires Are Projected On
The
3-D Waking Screen. [63]

Desires
Are Projected On The
3-D Dream Screen. [64]

Desires
Are Buried Deep In The
3-D Sleep Screen. [65]

Every Desire Is Nothing
But The Search For The
Impossible Pleasure. [66]

In Waking, Turiya
Becomes Ignorant As
The Waker.
Yet Turiyatita Remains
Ever Untainted And Bliss
Itself. [67]

In Dream, Turiya
Becomes Ignorant As
The Dreamer.
Yet Turiyatita Remains
Ever Untainted And Bliss
Itself. [68]

In Deep Sleep, Turiya
Becomes Ignorant As
The Sleeper.
Yet Turiyatita Remains
Ever Untainted And Bliss
Itself. [69]

Can The Waking State
Exist Without The
Presence Of
The Waker? [70]

Can The Waker
Prove That When He Is
Not In It, The Waking
State Still Exists? [71]

Can The Dreamer
Provide Evidence Of
The Existence Of The
Waking State, In The
Absence Of
The Waker? [72]

Is Another Waker's Testament, To The Existence Of The Waking State In Your Absence, Valid? [73]

Isn't A Waker,
Who Is Providing The
Testimony,
Of The Waking State's
Existence Without You,
A Part Of
Your Waking? [74]

Can The Waker
Be Independent Of The
Waking State?
Can The Waking State Be
Independent Of The
Waker? [75]

Do You Sense Yourself
As A Person Or Simply
The Presence Of
Awareness? [76]

Aren't The Waker
And The Waking State
Simply One And The
Same Single Illusion? [77]

Aren't The Dreamer
And The Dream State
Simply One And The
Same Single Illusion?[78]

Aren't The Deep Sleeper
And The Deep Sleep
State Simply One And
The Same Single
Illusion?[79]

Aren't The First, The Second, The Third And The Fourth Simply ONENESS? [80]

Can Turiya Be The
Waker?
Can Turiya Be The
Dreamer?
Can Turiya Be The
Sleeper?
Isn't It All Simply
Illusion? [81]

Who Is Projecting?
Waker? Dreamer? Deep
Sleeper? Turiya?
Or Turiyatita? [82]

Can There Exist True Happiness In the Three Worlds Or Is The Idea Of Happiness Simply Illusory? [83]

Isn't Turiyatita,
Sat
[Ultimate Truth],
Chid
[Pure Consciousness],
Ananda
[Beyond Happiness And
Unhappiness]? [84]

Could Turiyatita Be The Higher Witness? [85]

Where Is Knowing
Happening?
Who Is The Knower?
Waker? Dreamer?
Sleeper? Turiya?
Turiyatita? [86]

Who Am I? [87]

The Belief That
'I Am The Person'
Is An Obstacle To Seeing
The Truth. [88]

The Belief That
'I Am Born In A Pre-
existing World'
Is An Obstacle To Seeing
The Truth. [89]

The Belief That
'I Am The
Doer/Experiencer' Is An
Obstacle To Seeing The
Truth. [90]

The Belief That
It Is All About 'I' Versus
The 'Other'
Is An Obstacle To Seeing
The Truth. [91]

The Belief That
'The Fulfillment Of A
Desire Will Bring
Happiness'
Is An Obstacle To Seeing
The Truth. [92]

Until The Illusion Of
The Person Lasts,
The Truth Of
Turiyatita Will
Not Be Revealed. [93]

Until The Illusion Of
Ownership Lasts,
The Truth Of
Turiyatita Will Not Be
Revealed. [94]

Until The Illusion Of
Doership Lasts,
The Truth Of Turiyatita
Will Not
Be Revealed. [95]

Until The Illusion Of
Experiencership Lasts,
The Truth Of Turiyatita
Will Not
Be Revealed. [96]

If There Is No Doer,
No Experiencer,
No Thinker,
No Person,
Then Who Is The 'I'
That Claims Their
Ownership? [97]

Can The 'I' Exist By Itself? [98]

Is There A Self?
Is There A Non-Self?
Or
Is There Simply
Emptiness? [99]

I Am Yet I Am Not.
It Is Yet It Is Not.
All Is Awake Yet In Deep
Sleep! [100]

The Beginning!

Mentorship for Swapna Nidra Gnyana Sadhana is available at the upcoming Retreat.
Email: AncientWisdomPearls@Gmail.Com
Website: https://ektabathija.com/

Made in the USA
Monee, IL
16 October 2024

67795384R00062